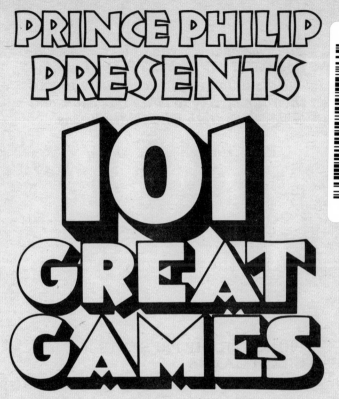

PRINCE PHILIP PRESENTS 101 GREAT GAMES

PAUL JAMES & PETER HESELTINE

Illustrated by Peter Stevenson

All Royalties to the National Playing Fields Association

A Carousel Book
Transworld Publishers Ltd.

*The National Playing Fields Associa-
tion would like to thank Peter Heseltine
and Paul James for generously giving
their time freely to write this book, and
Gyles Brandreth whose idea it was.*

PRINCE PHILIP PRESENTS 101
GREAT GAMES

A CAROUSEL BOOK 0 552 54246 6

First published in Great Britain by
Carousel Books 1983

PRINTING HISTORY
Carousel edition published 1983

Carousel Books are published by
Transworld Publishers Ltd.
Century House,
61—63 Uxbridge Road,
Ealing, London W.5.

Made and printed by
The Guernsey Press Co. Ltd., Channel Islands.

FOREWORD

by H.R.H. The Prince Philip, Duke of
Edinburgh, KG, KT

The National Playing Fields Association exists to
promote and provide places and opportunities for
children to play wherever they are most needed, and
the money raised by this book will be used to provide
more facilities. But places and opportunities are not
enough by themselves; they are only there so that
children can have the fun of playing games. In this
book there are 101 games. Some are very simple, others
are more complicated and demand greater skill, but
they are all to be enjoyed. If you know a favourite game
not included in this book, send it in, others might like to
know about it. If enough good games are suggested it
might be possible to produce a sequel to this book,
'Prince Philip Introduces Your Favourite Games'.

Send your games to: National Playing Fields
Association,
25 Ovington Square,
LONDON, SW3 ILQ

INTRODUCTION

The **101 GREAT GAMES** in this book are a mixture of both old and new. Some of them are old favourites that you will no doubt have played before, but most of them, we hope, will be completely fresh to you. You will find games for every occasion too. Some you can play when you are alone, perhaps if you happen to be ill in bed or even in hospital, whilst others can be played with your friends. Whether it is a sunny day on the beach, a birthday party at home, or a rainy day that keeps you inside, you will be able to find an exciting game to amuse you.

To help you choose which games to play, we have invented a simple code:

 are games that can be played by one person.

 are games that can be played by two people.

 are games that can be played by four or more.

are games that can be played by six or more with the help of a referee.

Many of the games for larger groups will be suitable for playing at school, in the playground or on playschemes. The final game is a personal challenge especially for you!

We hope that you will enjoy playing **101 GREAT GAMES**!

Game Number 1

USE YOUR SCENTS!

Let's begin with a game that can be played with any number of people and is ideal for a party. To set up the game you begin by exploring with your nose! Collect together ten different items that have a very distinctive smell. If it is Summer you can perhaps gather together different flower petals. Or at any time of the year explore the kitchen where you will find such things as onions, carrots, herbs, lemon, ginger, all of which have a very strong scent.

Get some match boxes and punch a hole in the top of each one, and carefully hide something that gives off a strong scent inside. The object of the game is to challenge your friends to try and identify what is inside the box using only their nose. The person to guess each scent correctly is the winner.

Why is your nose in the middle of your face?

Because it is the scenter! (Centre)

Game Number 2

MIND YOUR STEP

The next time you are out for a walk or on your way to the shops, why not make your expedition more fun by playing a game on the way?

There is a belief that if you step on a crack in the pavement, you kill a fairy. Some say that you could turn into a frog! Whatever you believe, as you walk along the pavement avoid treading on the cracks where the paving stones join and step very carefully so that you foot lands firmly in the centre of the square. It's not as easy as it sounds! With a little practice you might be able to do it with your eyes looking straight ahead and not at your feet.

Once you have mastered the art of avoiding the cracks, try it with a silly walk. First, hop six times on your left foot so that you land on a different paving stone each time, then six times on your right, six times on your left backwards, and six times on your right backwards. You can try this with a friend too, the winner being the one who can do it without stepping on any cracks.

What wears shoes but has no feet?

The pavement!

PULL-ME-UP

This game is a test of strength. Take a partner and sit on the floor facing each other with the soles of your feet touching. Now grasp hands and attempt to pull each other into a standing position. You may find it easier if you bend your knees, but if you are really fit keep your legs outstretched.

The object of the game is to pull the other person up whilst remaining seated yourself. The winner will be the strongest of the two that manages to remain seated. Try it also using only one hand instead of two, whilst reciting the alphabet **backwards**!

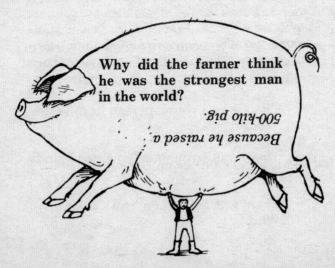

Why did the farmer think he was the strongest man in the world?

Because he raised a 500-kilo pig.

Game Number 4

LEERING LIMERICKS

Do you like limericks? One of the greatest limerick writers was a gentleman called **Edward Lear**. He wrote hundreds of them. He also wrote lots of very famous poems that you will probably know already, such as *'The Jumblies'*, *'The Yongy-Bongy-Bo'*, *'The Dong with a Luminous Nose'*, and of course *'The Owl and the Pussy Cat'*. If you haven't read them, try and find a book of Lear's verse in your library.

Here's one of Edward Lear's limericks:

> *There was an old man in a tree,*
> *Who was horribly bored by a bee;*
> *When they said: 'Does it buzz?'*
> *He replied: 'Yes, it does!*
> *It's a regular brute of a bee!'*

Now see if you can write some limericks of your own. Here are the first lines of three limericks for you to finish yourself:

There was a young person from Wales
Who. . . .

There was a young lady named Mandy
Who. . . .

There was a small boy with a dog
Who. . . .

Game Number 5

ASSAULT COURSE

Get together with some friends and gather as many objects as you can to make an assault course in your garden. Old cardboard boxes, rubber tyres, barrels, ropes, tea chests, and anything else that you can find which you can jump over, swing on, climb through, climb over, and so on.

When you have gathered all the items, set them out in a suitable part of your garden where they are not going to be in anybody's way, and make sure that **everything** is perfectly safe. If you have a wooden crate, for example, make certain there are no sharp nails sticking out of it. You might be able to involve your teacher or playleader in building an assault course at your school or local play area.

11

Set out the course so that each of your friends knows exactly what to do. For example, you might have to start by crawling through a cardboard box, jump over a rope, climb through a tyre that is hanging from a tree, squeeze through a barrel, run twice around a pile of twigs, and end up by jumping two metres over two pieces of string that you are pretending marks a deep river.

Once you have planned the course, each player must attempt it one at a time. The champion will be the one to complete the course in the shortest amount of time. Have someone act as a referee to check the timings. To make it even harder you can suggest that each player carries a balloon with them. If it bursts, they are disqualified.

**What is worse than a
turtle with claustrophobia?**

An elephant with a blocked nose.

Game Number 6

BLOW FOOTBALL

An exciting game for which you will need a lot of breath is the simple game of 'Blow Football'. All you need is a ping-pong or table-tennis ball, and two ordinary drinking straws.

The two players stand at opposite ends of a table. One player places the ball on the table and by blowing it with his straw attempts to blow it off the other end. You score a point each time you manage to get the ball over your opponent's end of the table. He in turn must blow with his straw to try and prevent you scoring, and in turn try and blow the ball over your end of the table so that he can score a point. If you happen to blow the ball off the side of the table, your opponent gets a free go.

The game can be played with four people, with one person on each side of the table. A more difficult version of the game is to play it on the floor instead of a table. Use a large sheet of newspaper to mark out the playing area.

Why was Cinderella thrown out of the blow football team?

Because she kept leaving the ball.

Game Number 7

RESEARCH PROJECT

This is a great game to play if you are on holiday in a particular town or are visiting a foreign country. Pretend that you are an investigator and conduct a research project on the town or area in question. What you should do is get a folder and fill it with a whole range of information, including a map, picture postcards, leaflets, your own drawings and notes. If you visit the local library and the nearest tourist information office and if you talk to local people, you will be able to discover a great deal. Here are some of the questions to which your research will provide the answers:

1) What is the history of the town or region?
2) Have any famous people lived in the area?
3) Are there any historic monuments?
4) Are there any strange local customs?
5) What is the population of the town or area?
6) How many schools does it have?
7) What are its main industries?
8) How many churches are there?
9) How many theatres and cinemas?
10) What is the favourite local food?
11) What is the weather like?
12) What is the geography of the area?

When you have answered these questions, and drawn lots of sketches and pictures, you will have a unique record of your visit, and can begin to build up a collection of similar files every time you go on holiday.

Why did the man put his coat on backwards?

Because he didn't know whether he was coming or going.

Game Number 8
COPYCAT

Here is a game that will test your reflexes and see how quickly you can react.

Begin by getting all the players to line up in a row facing you. They then have to imitate your every action. If you raise your right leg, they must raise their right legs. If you jump up and down, they must jump up and down. If you hold up the index finger of your left hand, they must do the same.

If any of the players makes a mistake, they must change places with you and become the person to be copied. Because you are **facing** them, it will not be long before you raise your right arm and one of the copycats will accidently raise their left arm, thinking that they are correct. See how quickly you can catch somebody out!

Game Number 9

STATUES

This game is ideal for parties when you have a large number of players, or try it in the playground with your schoolfriends. First choose a referee to see that there is fair play. One player stands in front of a wall with his or her back to the others. The other players stand in a line approximately twenty metres away.

The player facing the wall begins to recite:
> *'I think that I shall never see,*
> *A poem lovely as a brick.'*

as fast and loud as he or she can, while the other players move up slowly to try and touch the reciter. The moment the poem is finished, he or she wheels round and everyone must be standing as still as statues. If anyone is seen moving he or she is sent back to the starting line and must begin again. The players can only move when the poem is recited. The first person to touch the player at the wall is the winner and changes places.

Why does the Statue of Liberty stand in New York harbour?

Because she can't sit down.

Game Number 10

CODE BREAKER

An American named **Samuel Morse**, with the help of physicist **Joseph Henry**, invented a very special code that can be used to send messages by telegraph or light. Each letter of the alphabet has a code of dots and dashes, which can be tapped out or flashed with a torch. A short flash for a dot and a long flash for a dash. Once you have learnt the code you can send messages to your friends without anyone overhearing you.

The code is known as the **Morse Code** and looks like this:

A ·—	B —···	C —·—·	D —··	E ·	F ··—·
G ——·	H ····	I ··	J ·———	K —·—	L ·—··
M ——	N —·	O ———	P ·——·	Q ——·—	R ·—·
S ···	T —	U ··—	V ···—	W ·——	X —··—
Y —·——	Z ——··				
1 ·————	2 ··———	3 ···——	4 ····—		5 ·····
6 —····	7 ——···	8 ———··	9 ————·		0 —————

Secret messages can also be tapped out, or written.

Send this special message to your friend
and see if he can decode it. Then get him to
send a message back to you.

.— — /. . ../.—/—//—..//— — —//— .— —/— —
—/..—//—.—./.—/

.—..).— ..//.—//..— ./.— ./— — —/— — .//...).
— —./—.— —//?

.—//—.— ./.—./— — —/.—/— .—//.—/— .—
..//—..).—/— — /— — /

./.—//.—/— — —./ /—/—//

How do you make anti-freeze?

Steal her blanket.

Game Number 11

TOUCH/NOT TOUCH

A wide area is necessary for this game, and the more players you have the better. You will need one paper plate to every six players. So, if twenty-four people are playing, you will need four plates.

To start the game, the plates are placed on the ground and each of the six players must touch the plate **without touching any of the other players**. A wall or some other object is then chosen as 'home', and on the shout of 'GO!' from the referee everybody must run and touch 'home' and return to the plate as quickly as possible. While they are away the referee must remove one plate. Eventually you will get down to one plate — but remember that each player must touch the plate without touching any of the other players. If two players happen to touch, they must leave the game. The person left at the end is the winner.

To make the game even more exciting, someone can be chosen as 'wolf'. He or she must run and touch as many people as possible between the plate and 'home'. Whoever he or she touches leaves the game. The person left at the end takes over as 'wolf'.

Game Number 12

LEG WRESTLING

Are your legs strong? Put them to the test in a leg wrestling match.

First, remove your shoes so that you can wrestle in your stockinged feet. Lie on your back with your partner opposite you. Link your legs at the back of the knees. The aim of the game is to wrestle your opponent onto his or her side. Attempt to keep your back and arms flat against the floor throughout.

Which disease makes you much better at sport?

Athlete's foot.

Game Number 13

WALL BALL

As the name suggests, all you need for this game are a wall and a ball. Make sure it is a wall that has no windows or doors in it.

To play the game, throw the ball so that it bounces off the wall and back through your legs. Give yourself a point every time the ball goes through, and take a point off each time you miss.

When you are an expert challenge a friend to a game. You have to throw the ball at the wall and your friend has to jump in so that it bounces back through his or her legs. Take it in turns to throw the ball. The one with the highest number of points at the end of the game is the champion.

When is cricket a crime?

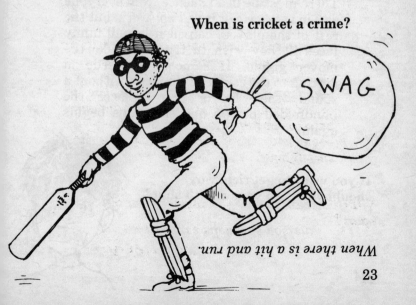

SWAG

When there is a hit and run.

Game Number 14

QUIET PLEASE!

An excellent party game for any number of players. Sit everyone in a very large circle and put one player in the centre. The person who has been chosen to sit in the centre must be blindfolded. He or she must then point to someone in the circle, and this person must get to the centre of the circle without making a single noise.

The blindfolded player will listen for a rustle of clothes, a footfall, heavy breathing, giggling, and if he or she hears any sound at all the other player must return to the edge of the circle and begin again. There must be dead silence from everyone else in the circle or it will not work, but the rest of the players can silently pull funny faces if they wish to try and make the mover giggle. If someone succeeds in getting to the centre of the circle without a sound, then he or she replaces the blindfolded person and the game begins again.

If you want to get rich, why should you keep your mouth shut?

Because silence is golden.

24

Game Number 15

SCRAMBLED LETTERS

You've heard of scrambled eggs, which are eggs that have been well mixed up. Here are some scrambled words, in which the letters have been all jumbled up. Can you try and unscramble them? A clue is that all the words may be found in the High Street.

a) TUBHERC

b) SHOOKPOB

c) YAKBER

d) AUNTRATSER

e) INORMNOMREG

f) GGAARE

g) MISTCHE

h) SSRCOZGNIRABE

i) KBNA

j) SUBPOST

k) CHUBOILSUPE

l) AAIRTKNX

m) STTAEIONR

n) YMRAGNITUIRCERECIFFO

o) LICETATPOSION

p) FISTROL

q) VELENTAARGT

r) TLRIAGFHFTISC

s) TEKMARREPUS

t) EEGGEORRRNC

When you have unscrambled them, try them out on your friends.

Solutions

a) Butcher   b) Bookshop   c) Bakery
d) Restaurant   e) Ironmonger
f) Garage   g) Chemist
h) Zebra Crossing   i) Bank
j) Bus Stop   k) Public House
l) Taxi Rank   m) Stationer
n) Army Recruiting Office
o) Police Station   p) Florist
q) Travel Agent   r) Traffic Lights
s) Supermarket   t) Greengrocer

A man had two sons and called them both Ed. Why?

Because two Eds are better than one.

Game Number 16

WHEELIES

This is a game that can be played in pairs, and once you have learnt the art of doing it properly you can even have a wheelies race.

First, find some grass or nice soft mats to try this on so that there is no danger of anybody hurting themselves. Remove your shoes and socks too before you begin. Get your partner to lay flat on the ground facing upwards. You then lay on top of your partner **the wrong way round** so that you are both grasping each others ankles. You must now try and change places like a wheel! If you both hold tightly to your partner's ankles, and the person on top goes head over heels you'll find it's easy.

The game is much easier if you find a partner who is the same height and weight as yourself.

FRIENDLY FLOWERS

Have you noticed how the names of certain objects and animals can often sound like people's names? For example, **mistletoe** can sound like **Miss. L. Toe**, or an **antelope** could be a little girl called **Ann T. Lope**! There are hundreds more names, such as **Nora Bone, Miss D. Bus, Ivor Clue, Bill Ding, Rhoda Camel, Neil Down, Gail Force, Dinah Mite, I. Forgot,** and **Milly Metre**! All of which come from everyday words and phrases.

Flowers especially can sound like real people. Here are a few examples — can you think up some more?

Lu Pin and Fu Schia, the Chinese Acrobats.
Dan de Lion, the French Knight
and his Horse Chestnut.
Mary Gold and June Iper,
the dancing duo.
P. Pod and his Dog
Rose.

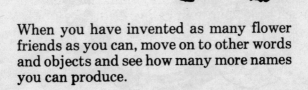

When you have invented as many flower friends as you can, move on to other words and objects and see how many more names you can produce.

Game Number 18

CIRCLE CROSS

If someone in your group has a loud voice then they will be ideal for this game, because you need one person to be the caller who can shout very loudly.

All the players stand in a large circle, and are numbered alternately by the caller . 1 . 2 . 1 . 2 . 1 . 2 . and so on around the circle until everybody has been given either the number 1 or the number 2. When each person knows his or her number, all the players must then kneel down in the circle.

When everyone is kneeling, the caller begins to shout out numbers 1 or 2, or 1, 1, 1, 2, 1, 2, 1, 2, 2 and so on. Each time your number is called you are able to move one part of your body, such as a foot or a hand. The idea of the game is to change sides in the circle, one movement at a time. This sounds simple until everyone begins to reach the centre, then the problems begin! You will have to work out ways of climbing over or round, or under the other players. Remember, you can only make one move each time your number is called.

PUSH-UPS

Choose a partner who is about the same
size as yourself and stand facing each other
with the palms of your hands together.
Take a step backwards so that you are lean-
ing on each other. Working together, try to
push yourselves back into an upright position simply by pushing with your palms.

When you have mastered that, try it again
with three of you in a triangular formation.
That is much more difficult to do without
moving your feet. The more people who
join in, the more you will have to co-operate
with each other to be able to do the game.

**Who has the strongest fingers
in the world?**

*A miser because he is always
pinching pennies.*

Game Number 20

FOOT PAINTING

This game is tremendous fun, but **very messy** so wear your oldest clothes and play it outside if you can.

You will need some large sheets of paper — old wallpaper or shelf lining paper is ideal, but newspaper will be fine if that is all you have. Use an old baking tray or large flat dish, and mix up some water based powder or poster paint in it. Use nice bright colours if you can.

Now comes the fun part! Remove your shoes and socks and dip one of your feet into the paint. Go for a walk across your blank sheet of paper and you will end up with a line of coloured footprints. Wash your foot in a bowl of clean water, and then dip your other foot in a different colour and walk across the paper again so that you build up a pattern of alternate colour footprints.

See what different patterns you can make by walking on tip-toe or on your heels. You will be surprised at the amazing pictures you can create. You can do similar paintings by using the palms of your hands as well. Always use water based paints though, as these will wash off easily.

Why shouldn't you believe painters?

Because they spread it on thick!

HOLD TIGHT!

Here is a very simple game that will be a real test of your sense of balance.

You need a low platform each to stand on — a large log of wood, a small crate, or an upturned bucket would be ideal — and about 6 metres of rope. Place the two platforms about 3 metres apart.

To play the game, each player squats on his or her platform holding on to one end of the rope. Start to reel your end of the rope in until it becomes tight, and then try to unbalance the other person by pulling or letting go of the rope. It's rather like a tug of war, except you are trying to make your opponent step down from their platform.

If it is a hot Summer's day, play the game with each platform on either side of a paddling pool and pull away! Do wear your swimming costume though, because one of the players is going to get wet!

Is it dangerous to swim on a full stomach?

Yes, it's better to swim in water.

KNOTTY

Knot knonsense, knotorious or knote-worthy, but knoticably the knottiest of knots ever knotted!

The object of this game is to tie a human knot. The referee or person supervising the game should stand all the players in a circle facing each other. Everyone places their hands in the centre of the circle and grabs hold of another hand. The two hands that you grab must each belong to different people, and you are not allowed to take the hand of the person standing next to you.

When everybody is holding hands you will find that you have made one big knot! All you have to do now is untangle the knot **without letting go** so that you end up back in one big circle again. Knot easy is it! The referee must watch to make sure that nobody lets go.

What do you call a person who doesn't have all his fingers on one hand?

Normal. Fingers are supposed to be on two hands.

33

Game Number 23

HOW SQUARE!

If you are going on a journey in a car, coach, train or plane, then occupy the time by playing a game with one of your travelling companions.

To play this game you will need to make up a grid of dots, like this:

```
.   .   .   .   .   .   .   .   .
.   .   .   .   .   .   .   .   .
.   .   .   .   .   .   .   .   .
.   .   .   .   .   .   .   .   .
.   .   .   .   .   .   .   .   .
```

Taking it in turns you each put in one line at a time, either across or downwards (not diagonally), so that you gradually build up a grid of squares. The aim is to complete the fourth side of a square on your turn, because if you are the one that completes a square you put your initial in it and have another go.

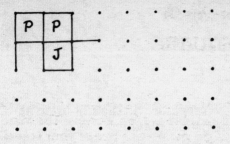

You must try and stop your opponent from completing a square. The one with the most squares when the grid is completed is the winner. As you approach the end of the game you will find it gets more and more difficult to put in a line without giving your opponent a square.

Game Number 24

I LIKE TREES

This word game will the test brain power of all the people playing!

Begin the game by standing in front of the other players, and give them a list of things that you do and don't like:

I like trees, but I don't like flowers.
I like grass, but I don't like leaves.
I like football, but I don't like cricket.
I like Liverpool, but I don't like London.
I like otters, but I don't like beavers.

Have you noticed what is special about those likes and dislikes? Everything 'I like' contains two vowels or two consonants side by side — trEEs, graSS, fOOtball, LiverpOOl, oTTers — and all the things 'I don't like' don't.

As soon as one of the other players spots this, he or she must interrupt you and tell you what he or she likes and dislikes. If he or she has got the idea they will come and stand at your side and say something like:

I like yeLLow, but I don't like orange.
I like bEEf, but I don't like pork.

The last player to catch on to the idea is the loser and chooses the next game to play.

Play the game another way by choosing words that all have a certain vowel in, or words that all end in '-ing', words like 'sight' and 'site' that sound the same but have a different meaning, and see who is first to spot the system.

Which has more legs, a horse or no horse?

No horse. A horse has four legs but no horse has six legs.

Game Number 25

ANIMALS

If you are having a party, this silly but fun game will really get everybody in the party mood.

Collect all the players together and ask them to close their eyes. When their eyes are tightly closed, give each player a number — either, 1, 2 or 3. Mix everyone around so that they are all standing in various parts of the room.

Tell them that number one's have got to make noises like a pig; number two's must imitate a cow; number three's must pretend that they are dogs! Keeping their eyes shut they have got to get themselves into three groups simply by making animal noises, so that all the pigs end up in a group together, all the cows in another part of the room, and all the dogs in the final group. Keep your eye on them so that no 'animal' bumps into any furniture.

Tell your three groups these jokes!

Why are most cows noisy?

Because they have horns.

Why did the pigs leave home?

Because their father was a big boar (bore).

Why does a dog have fur?

Because if it didn't it would be a little bear (bare).

Game Number 26

CATCH IT

This game has nothing to do with germs! You simply have to catch three objects — except it isn't really all that simple!

Get your friend to stand on a chair or stool and drop an ordinary **sheet of writing paper** from a great height. All you have to do is catch the piece of paper between your finger and thumb before it reaches the ground. Easy? Try it and find out!

Next get your friend to drop a **blown-up balloon** for you. You must catch it with **one** hand only.

Finally, get the person to drop some **curtain rings** or small hoops, which you must catch on **one** finger.

Now change places with your friend, and see who is the best at catching all the objects.

Game Number 27

WHAT IS IT?

In Exeter Cathedral Library in Devon there is an old manuscript of riddles which is thought to be over 1,000 years old. Here are two examples of riddles:

1) *In my watery world I flash like gold*
   Hard to catch, harder to hold.
   When danger comes I go with speed
   Into the safe and watery weed.

2) *Furry, purry, ginger or tabby*
   My coat is never shabby.
   Sleekly shines this coat of hairs
   As I wash behind my ears.

Could you work out the answers? They were easy, weren't they. Riddles are still just as popular today. Here are some modern ones for you to guess. See if you can make up some of your own, and try them on your friends.

3) *If you feed it,*
   It will live;
   If you give it water,
   It will die.

4) *Six legs, two heads,*
   Two hands and a nose.
   But uses only four legs as it goes.
   What is it?

5) *What is it,*
   A rich man has and wants more of,
   A fat man has and doesn't want,
   And a poor man wants and can't get?

6) *A skin have I,*
   More eyes than one.
   I can be nice when I am done.
   What am I?

Solutions
1) A fish 2) A cat 3) Fire 4) A man on horseback 5) Pounds 6) A potato.

42

Game Number 28

SCAVENGER HUNT

During the school holidays, have a scavenger hunt with your friends. Set a certain amount of time for the hunt, and have all the players meet up again at a certain time. The one who has collected the most items on the list is the winner. Here is the list of items that the Scavenger Hunters must collect:

1. A used First Class stamp.
2. A 1983 penny.
3. A wrapped sugar lump.
4. A pebble that looks like a bird's egg.
5. A four-leafed clover.
6. An acorn.
7. A piece of silver foil, or milk-bottle top.
8. A ring-pull from a drinks can.
9. A piece of string 50cms long.
10. A bus ticket.
11. A postcard sent from a foreign country.
12. A used ticket from a museum or stately home.
13. An empty matchbox.
14. A foreign coin.
15. An elastic band.
16. A large cornflake.
17. A Supermarket carrier bag.
18. The name and address of a doctor in your town.
19. A pencil with a rubber attached to one end.
20. A cork.

Game Number 29

UP THE STAIRS

When you have practiced this game yourself, try it with some friends and see who
builds the biggest word stair. The game
involves building up a ladder of words like
this:

A

A T

A N T

A U N T

A N K L E

A N T L E R   AUNT

A N O T H E R

A S S A S S I N

A T R O C I O U S

A S P I R A T I O N

A S S I G N A T I O N

A C A N T H A C E O U S

A C C E L E R O M E T E R

A C C O M P L I S H M E N T

A C K N O W L E D G E M E N T

A C A N T H O P T E R Y G I A N

A E R O T H E R M O D Y N A M I C

A N T I F E R R O M A G N E T I S M

A D R E N O L O R T I C O T R O P I C

Up to ten letters you should be able to do yourself, but for the really long ones try hunting through a dictionary. Work your way through the alphabet, producing a word stair for **B, C, D,** and so on.

What time of day was Adam born?

A little before Eve.

Game Number 30

SILHOUETTE

A silhouette is a portrait in profile or outline in black on a white background. In Victorian times it was a popular hobby to cut out silhouettes from black card and paste them onto a sheet of white paper. These were then framed and used to decorate their rooms, in much the same way that we frame photographs of people today.

To make your very own silhouettes, pin or Blue-tac a piece of paper onto a wall. Get a friend to sit in front of it, and shine a strong light from a lamp in front of your friend so that the shadow of his or her head falls on the paper. Draw carefully around the outline of the shadow and fill it in with black paint, and you will have a perfect silhouette of your friend. Now get him or her to make one of you.

To see how successful you are at making silhouettes, show them to your family and see if they recognise who the pictures are of. If they can identify the silhouettes, then your efforts were a success!

DAD

ME **What is dark but made by light?**

A shadow.

MUM

FIDO

THUMBS DOWN

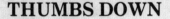

Have you ever thought how useful your thumbs are? Most of us tend to take our thumbs for granted; they are there next to our fingers, we suck them when we are babies, we stick them in the air when we approve of something, they enable you to count up to ten on your hands, and if you're like Little Jack Horner you can stick your thumb in a pie and pull out a plum! But do you use them for anything else? If you had not realised how important your thumbs are to you, this game will show you exactly how much you use them.

Take a piece of sticky tape and tape your thumb and first fingers together. If you are right-handed tape the thumb on your right hand, and the left thumb if you are left-handed.

Now carry on as if nothing had happened, but everytime you find that something has become very hard to do because of your lack of thumb, write it down. You'll be surprised at how long your list will become . . . that is if you can write without a thumb.

Try doing up your buttons, peeling a banana, picking up a ball, blowing your nose or comb your hair, without using your thumb. It is so difficult that it is almost impossible.

Game Number 32

BAT-A-RAT

Wild (Tame ones are) rats are not very pleasant creatures, but you are not going to use a real rat for this game, so don't worry! Use a small rubber ball or a bean bag, and pretend that it is a rat. You will also need to make a cardboard tube about 1.5 metres long, which will act as a drainpipe for your 'rat' to crawl down.

Place a bucket or bowl on the ground and get someone to stand 3 metres away from it holding the tube. The person holding the tube will slide the rat down the tube, and as it appears at the other end the players must take it in turns to hit the rat with a bat, and knock it into the bucket. They score a point each time they get the rat in the bucket. It is much more difficult than it sounds because the players cannot tell exactly when the 'rat' will appear and when it does come out the end of the tube they will have to act very quickly to knock it into the bucket.

When does a rat weigh as much as an elephant?

When the scales are broken.

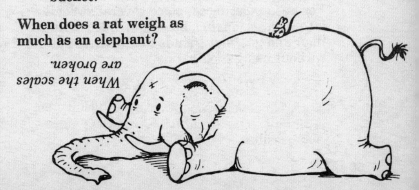

Game Number 33

PALE FACE

Why did the Red Indian's face go white when he blushed?

Because he was a Pale Face.

No, this game has nothing to do with Red Indians, but you could end up with some pale faces if you play this at your next party.

Take a very large baking tray and put on it a mound of flour. Balance a chocolate on top of the mound and then challenge someone to take the sweet off the top of the pile **with their mouth!**

For even paler faces, place several sweets into a large mixing bowl half filled with flour and get your friends to fish them out without using their hands.

Game Number 34

BALLOON TOSS

This very messy game must be played outside, preferably on a warm day. Try it the very next time you are on the beach with your friends.

Fill some balloons half-full with water and tie a knot in the neck so that the water cannot escape. The players should stand in two rows about a metre apart and facing each other. The balloon starts at one end and is tossed from one row to the other all the way down. If it reaches the bottom without bursting, both rows take one pace backwards and pass the balloon back again.

If the balloon bursts at any time a second balloon starts from where the first one burst. Each time the balloon gets from one end to the other without bursting, the rows take a pace backwards every time.

Keep the game going as fast as possible, but be sure that no-one is wearing their best clothes.

Game Number 35

SOUNDS SERIOUS

It is surprising how often you need to be able to see an action to identify the sound that goes with it. Try this game out on your family and friends to see how good they are at identifying sounds.

Collect all the items together that you will need and keep them in a box out of sight until you are ready to use them. Blindfold the other players, or simply get them to sit with their backs to you. As you make the sounds they must shout out what they think they are. They score a point for each correct answer. Alternatively you can get them all to write down what they think the sounds are.

These are the sounds you can make:

1. Flick through the leaves of a book.
2. Crumple up a sheet of newspaper.
3. Blow up a balloon.
4. Tear up a piece of paper.
5. Roll a marble around the inside of a bottle.
6. Place a spoon inside a glass.
7. Pour uncooked rice onto a tin tray.
8. Pour water from a jug into a paper cup.
9. Write on paper with a pencil.

10. Rub it out.
11. Draw your fingernail across a hardback book cover.
12. Blow bubbles through a straw.
13. Clean your teeth with a toothbrush.
14. Open a can of fizzy drink.
15. Snap your fingers.
16. Kiss the palm of your hand.
17. Rattle a box of matches.

Game Number 36

OLYMPIC GAMES

Gather together as many friends as you can and organise your very own Olympic Games. You will need plenty of space in which to play, such as a sports field, a large garden, or the beach. Mark a starting line and a finishing post for all your races, and get the referee to start the races off and see that there is no cheating! The person who wins the most events should be awarded with a prize.

Here are some ideas for different races you can stage as part of your Olympic Games:

1. A three-legged race with the players in pairs.

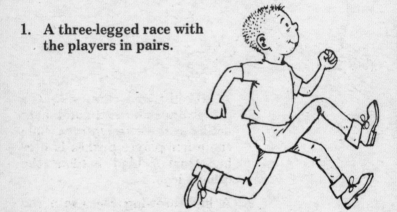

2. A hop-skip-and-jump race, in which the players have to hop, skip and jump their way along the course.

3. A backward race with all the players running backwards.

4. A hopping race, first using right feet only, then left feet only.

5. A head-over-heels race, with players somersaulting down the course.

6. A water race, with players carrying buckets of water and being disqualified if they spill any.

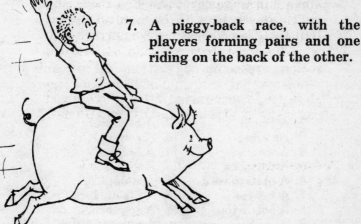

7. A piggy-back race, with the players forming pairs and one riding on the back of the other.

8. A wheelbarrow race, with the players in pairs and one player acting as the wheelbarrow, while the other player pushes him or her from behind holding the other's legs.

9. A ball-throwing race, with the players in pairs having to throw a ball from one to another as they race along the track. If a player drops a ball they are disqualified.

THE MEMORY GAME

Give each player a pencil and paper before you begin this game. You will then produce a tray on which you have set out twenty small objects. Let the players look at the objects for **one minute**, then cover the tray with a cloth. The players must then remember as many of the objects as they can and write them down on their paper. The person who can remember the most items is the winner.

Here are some suggestions for possible objects that you could have on your tray:

1. A matchbox
2. A pencil
3. An eraser
4. A watch
5. A teaspoon
6. A playing card
7. A toy car
8. A bottle top
9. A conker
10. A candle
11. A magnifying glass
12. A button
13. A comb
14. A lump of sugar
15. An ink bottle
16. A whistle
17. A plastic fork
18. A sea shell
19. A piece of string
20. An elastic band

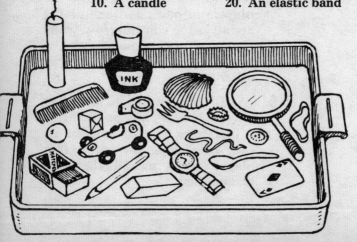

Game Number 38

SHOELACES

Find a pair of lace-up shoes and take the laces out. Each player should sit on the floor with a lace-less shoe behind their backs where it cannot be seen. Keeping the shoe behind them, and without looking, they must put the lace back in the shoe and tie a bow. The first to do this without looking or missing any holes out is the winner.

What runs around all day and then lies under your bed with its tongue hanging out?

Your shoe.

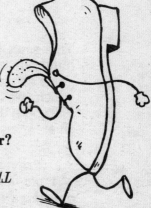

Why is a shoemaker like a minister?

They both try to save soles (souls).

Game Number 39

KING BY YOUR LEAVE

This game has been played by children for hundreds of years, and it is still a good game to play. In a document dated 1572, which was during the reign of Queen Elizabeth I, the game was described like this:

'A playe that children have, where one sytting blyndefolde in the midle, bydeth so tyll the rest have hydden themselves, and then he going to seeke them, if any get to his place in the meane space, that same is Kynge in his roome.'

The language is very different isn't it, but it is still easy to work out how to play the game, and it is ideal for a rainy day too. Whoever is the King should take the blindfold off before searching, otherwise he or she won't be able to find what he or she is looking for! Capture people by tagging, and take it in turns to act as referee.

Once upon a time there was a king.
Set before him were three glasses.
Two of them were filled with water.
The other one was empty. What
was the king's name?

Philip (fill up) the Third.

Game Number 40

MORE FAMOUS THAN BOTTICELLI

This favourite Victorian parlour game is still very popular today, and can be played by as few as two people, but is better with a larger number.

The object of the game is for one person to think of a famous person. For example, they might choose Captain Cook, the famous English navigator. The other players then have to ask questions to try and find out the person's identity. The game might go like this:

'Is the person living or dead?'
  'Dead.'
'Is it someone from fact or fiction?'
  'Fact.'

'Male or female?'
  'Male.'
'Was he a writer?'
  'No.'
'Was he a politician?'
  'No.'
'Was he an actor?'
  'No.'
'Was he an explorer?'
  'Yes.'

'Was he a sailor?'
  'Yes.'
'Was it Christopher
Columbus?'
  'No.'

and so the game continues with the players
taking it in turns to ask questions until
they discover the person's identity.

Game Number 41

SHOUTING PROVERBS

This is a lovely noisy game that is ideal for parties when a large number of people are present. The referee or person in charge splits the players into two teams. The first team is then secretly given a proverb, without the opposing team knowing what it is, and each person is given one word of that proverb. For example, you might choose:

A STITCH IN TIME SAVES NINE

and so the first member of the team would be given the word 'A', the next the word 'STITCH', and so on. If there are more players than words in your proverb, then give two people the same word.

The two teams then face each other and on a signal from the referee the first team all shout out their words at the same time, and the opposing team have to try and guess what the proverb or saying is. If they do not get it the first time, they are allowed two more shouts. If they still don't get it, the shouting team give themselves a point, and choose another proverb to shout. If the second team guess correctly, they score a point and take their turn at shouting a proverb. The first team to score six points is the winner.

The same game can be played by replacing proverbs with book titles, song titles, the names of plays or television programmes, with each player in the team shouting a different word of the title.

Game Number 42

THIMBLE RACE

An excellent team game for younger children to play. All you need are an ordinary drinking straw for each of the players, and two thimbles.

The players are divided up into two teams of equal numbers and put into two lines. Each team has a leader, who is given a thimble. On the word 'Go' from the referee, the leader puts his straw in his mouth and the thimble on top of the straw.

The leader turns to face the second player in the team, who will also have a straw in his or her mouth and will take the thimble on the end of his or her straw, and so pass it down the team. At no point can the thimble be touched by hand. If it is dropped on the floor at any time it must be returned to the leader and the team must begin again.

The game ends when one of the teams has successfully passed the thimble from one end of their team to the other and the last player has the thimble on the end of his or her straw. The team to finish first are the winners. If you only have small teams, the thimble can be passed from the leader down the row and then back up the row to the leader again.

Game Number 43

CROSSING THE RIVER

Here are two games that will really get your brain ticking over. See how quickly you can work out the solutions to these problems.

1) Three missionaries accompanied by three cannibals wish to cross a river. The problem is that they have a rowing boat which will only carry two people. How can they all get across the river without *at any time* there being *more* cannibals than missionaries on either side of the river?

2) Farmer Beasley wishes to take a fox, a chicken and a sack of corn across the river. The boat will only carry himself and *one* of the three across. Farmer Beasley's problem is that if he leaves the fox and the chicken together, the chicken will be eaten by the fox. If he leaves the chicken and the corn together, the chicken will eat the corn. How does Farmer Beasley get them all safely across the river?

Solutions:

1. **Journey One:** A missionary and a cannibal go over in the boat. The missionary returns, leaving the cannibal behind.
   Journey Two: Two cannibals cross, one remains, the other rows back.
   Journey Three: Two missionaries row over, a cannibal and a missionary row back.
   Journey Four: Two missionaries row over and a cannibal rows back.
   Journey Five: A cannibal rows over a cannibal and rows back.
   Journey Six: Two cannibals row over together.

2. **Journey One:** The farmer takes the chicken across and rows back.
   Journey Two: He rows over with the fox and rows back with the chicken.
   Journey Three: He rows over the corn, leaves it with the fox and returns for the chicken.

67

Game Number 44

HAND-IN, HAND-OUT

Another very old game which has a most interesting history, because in the fifteenth century King Edward IV passed a law which **banned children from playing it!** We can't think why, can you? Perhaps the King kept losing!

All the players stand together in a large circle, except one. The one remaining player creeps around the outside of the circle and touches one member of the circle on the back. The player who was touched must then leave the circle and chase the toucher until he is caught. The toucher can run either way around the outside of the circle, or dodge in and out of the other players to avoid being captured. When he or she is caught, the person who was touched then takes a turn of creeping around the circle and tapping someone on the back.

What goes around in circles and makes children happy?

A Merry-Go-Round.

READING IN REVERSE

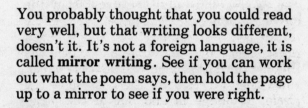

Some say that fleas are black,
But I know that is not so.
Because Mary had a little lamb
With fleas as white as snow.

You probably thought that you could read very well, but that writing looks different, doesn't it. It's not a foreign language, it is called **mirror writing**. See if you can work out what the poem says, then hold the page up to a mirror to see if you were right.

Now try it on your friends to see if they can do it. You can copy down some poems of your own in reverse writing, it's not easy to do, and then have a competition with your friends. The winner is the person who can read out the whole poem first, without looking in a mirror!

What turns everything around without even moving?

A mirror, of course!

Game Number 46

EVERYDAY SOUNDS

Below is a list of everyday sounds. What you have to do is imitate those noises with your voice, tongue and teeth as accurately as you can. Your friends must guess what the noises are. If they guess correctly you will have proof that you were making the right sounds. Each player scores a point for each sound that he guesses correctly. The players can take it in turns to make the different sounds.

Here are some noises to imitate:

1. A door creaking.
2. A clock being wound up.
3. A telephone dialling.
4. Gas escaping.
5. A grandfather clock ticking.
6. Footsteps on a country road.
7. A baby crying.
8. A trimphone ringing.
9. A vacuum cleaner.
10. A car starting.
11. A kettle boiling.
12. A bath being emptied.
13. A train.
14. A motorbike.
15. Someone sharpening a pencil.

GRANDFATHER CLOCK

OBADIAH

All the players should stand together in a line, one behind the other. The first person in the line says:

'My son Obadiah's going to be married, twiddle your thumbs.'

The next person in the line repeats this and does the action. As it starts on its way down the line the first person says:

'My son Obadiah's going to be married, scratch your head,' and that is passed down the line.

Then the first player says:

'My son Obadiah's going to be married, fall on one knee.'

This is repeated one at a time by the others and they do the action one at a time. You can add as many actions as you like.

Finish the game by saying:

'My son Obadiah's going to be married, do as you see me do.' then all fall down like a row of dominoes.

Game Number 48

FANNING THE KIPPER

Cut some 'kipper' shapes out of tissue paper and give one to each of the players, together with a magazine or comic.

Place a row of paper plates at one end of the room and get the players to stand at the other end with the kipper on the floor in front of them.

On the shout of 'Go!' each player must fan his or her kipper with the magazine or comic, and waft it towards the plate. The winner is the first person to get a kipper onto their plate, without touching the kipper either with their hands or the magazine.

Why is a fish like a person who talks too much?

Because neither can keep their mouths shut.

Game Number 49

SADDLE THE NAG

Collect your friends together and get them to stand in a line, one behind the other. Ask them to bend their backs with their arms tightly around the person in front so that they look like one very long horse.

You have to make your way over the backs of your friends from one end to the other, astride them as if you were sitting on a horse, without being thrown off. You are allowed three goes, then you must change places with the person at the end of the horse and let them try.

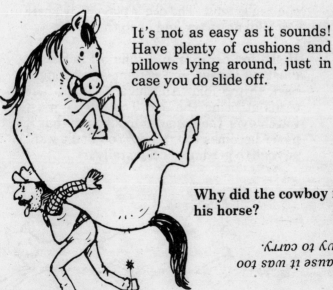

It's not as easy as it sounds! Have plenty of cushions and pillows lying around, just in case you do slide off.

Why did the cowboy ride his horse?

Because it was too heavy to carry.

73

FOX AND FOLD

A fairly boisterous game which is excellent to play on a very cold day when you need warming up, especially if the teachers send you out to play on an icy January breaktime.

One player is chosen to be the fox. The remaining players join hands around him or her to form a large circle, which is the fold. The fox is in the middle of the fold and has to try and escape by getting out of the circle. The fox must try and dash between someone's legs when they are not looking, or find a weak link in the circle so that he or she can get out. The other players, who are the fold, must try and keep the fox in.

If the fox escapes and runs off he or she must be chased and caught and brought back to the fold. All players should take turns at being the fox. The referee must watch over the game to make sure that it never becomes too rough. You don't want anyone to get hurt accidentally.

SOLO PING-PONG

A game of Ping-Pong is always fun, but what happens if you are on your own and have nobody to play it with you? Well, you can still play ping-pong by making a special bat.

Get an adult to help you with this. You will need a piece of plywood approximately 30 cms × 23 cms to which a piece of dowelling rod should be fixed, either by glueing or tacking. Fix two pieces of 10 cm dowling on either side by drilling and glueing and stretch a piece of muslin between, like this:

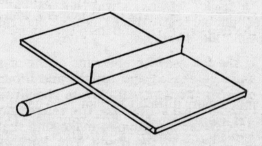

Now get a ping-pong ball and see how many times you can bounce it over the net without letting it bounce off the board.

Game Number 52

THE MINISTER'S CAT

This game was first seen played in Gloucestershire nearly one hundred years ago, and is excellent for wet afternoons or long journeys.

The first player begins by saying:
   'The Minister's cat was an Artful cat.'
The next player must think of another way of describing the cat, such as:
   'The Minister's cat was a Bumptious cat.'
the next player to have a go says:
   'The Minister's cat was a Clever cat.'
and so on right through the alphabet. X can be a tricky letter, so why not call it a Xenophobic cat — that means the cat doesn't like strangers.

A much more difficult version is to use different clergymen too. For example, *'The Archbishop's cat is an Affectionate cat,'* *'The Bishop's cat is a Boring cat,'* *'The Curate's cat is a Calculating cat,'* *'The Dean's cat is a Dangerous cat,'* and so on.

Yet another version is to give the cat's names, like this:

'*The Minister's cat is a Funny cat and his name is Fred.*'

'*The Minister's cat is a Glorious cat and his name is Gregory.*'

'*The Minister's cat is a Horrible cat and his name is Hubert.*'

'*The Minister's cat is an Inquisitive cat and his name is Idris.*'

Game Number 53

ORANGES AND LEMONS

You must know the old song **Oranges and Lemons**, but have you heard this version from Northamptonshire?

> *Pancakes and Fritters*
> *Say the bells of St. Peter's.*
> *Where must we fry them?*
> *Say the bells of Cold Higham;*
> *In yonder land furrow,*
> *Say the bells of Wellingborough.*
> *You owe me a shilling,*
> *Say the bells of Great Billing;*
> *When will you pay me?*
> *Say the bells of Middleton Cheney;*
> *When I am able,*
> *Say the bells of Dunstable;*
> *That will never be,*
> *Say the bells of Coventry;*
> *Oh, yes, it will,*
> *Says Northampton Great Bill;*
> *White bread and sop,*
> *Say the bells of Kingsthorpe;*
> *Trundle a lantern,*
> *Say the bells at Northampton.*

Using a map, if you need to, make up a rhyme like this for the churches and towns in your own area, following the same pattern as 'Oranges and Lemons, say the bells of St. Clements. . . .'

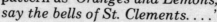

Game Number 54

TIP-IT

There are many similar versions of this game, but an old favourite is to split the players into two teams. Each team sit down at a table facing each other.

A ring or a similar small object is taken by the first side who put their hands under the table and one person takes the ring. The players then return their hands to the table and the other side must guess which hand is holding the ring. They order what they think are the empty hands off the table one at a time, by saying: *'Michael remove your right hand. Now Fiona take away your left hand. Sally remove your left hand . . .'* and so on, until only one hand is left. On the order of *'Tip-It'* the last hand is opened. If the guess is right the ring changes sides, if not the same team have another go. The object of the game is for your team to hang on to the ring as long as possible.

A more difficult version of the game is for the players to lay their hands palm downwards on the table with the ring under one person's hand. The opposing team can say *'Pass the ring'* as many times as they like, in which case you must all move your hands together to try and cover up which hand is passing the ring.

A final version is that of threading the ring on a loop of string. One player stands in the middle and the others stand in a circle with their hands clasped over the string. They must then pass the ring around the string from hand to hand until the player in the middle guesses correctly where the ring is.

**What kind of music does
a ghost like?**

Haunting melodies.

PUZZLE SQUARES

Make these two puzzle squares out of cardboard. You can carry them around with you in your pocket to play at any time, or challenge your friends to try them.

To make the first puzzle square, take a piece of card and cut it into four pieces like this:

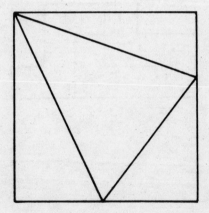

Jumble the four triangles up and then try to reassemble them into a square again.

The second puzzle is much more difficult. Take another square and cut it up into these eight shapes. Mix them all up and then try to put the square back together again. It's quite hard to do because the shapes look very much alike. When you have mastered it, get a friend to attempt it.

BIRDS, BEASTS AND FISHES

With just a pencil and paper this game can keep you occupied on a long journey for hours.

The first player writes down the first and last letter of a bird's, beast's and a fish's name, making crosses instead of the other letters like this:

```
S  x  x  x  x  x  x  x  x  H
E  x  x  x  x  x  x  x  T
O  x  x  x  x  x  H
```

The other player has to guess what the name is. They do this by calling out up to five letters which have to be put in where the crosses are if they are guessed correctly. After five letters they must try and guess the whole word. To make it a little easier, if you wish, you can say which word is the bird, which the beast and fish. For example, in the above, if you were told that the bottom word is the bird, you can soon guess that it is an ostrich. Can you work out the others?

What fish do pelicans eat?

Anything that fits the bill.

83

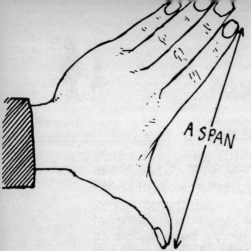

A SPAN

BANGER

This is an old London street game, which is also played in America but is known there as 'Spans'.

To play the game you will need some tiddly-winks or buttons. One player puts a button on the ground near a wall. The other player snaps a button into the air, as in the game of tiddlywinks, so that it goes up against the wall. If the button drops within one hand span (the distance between the thumb and first finger outstretched) of the button laid down, score 2 points. Within two spans, score 1 point. When it hits the button and bounces within one span it counts as 4, within two spans 3, and over that 2. Each player snaps in turn up to 20 points — the first one to reach the target wins.

If you add 2-forget and 2-forget, what do you get?

4-gotten.

THE PLATE GAME

This is a simple little game which only takes a minute or two to prepare. Make a ring of cardboard about 30 cms in diameter and cut out of it a hole approximately 20 cms in diameter. Stick it to the centre of a paper plate and place a large marble on the plate. Holding the plate in one hand only, try to get the marble into the hole.

Knock, Knock.
Who's there?
Hair.
Hair who?
Hair today, gone tomorrow.

Game Number 59

MOANING RULER

This has nothing to do with pretending to be a miserable king, it is instead a method of making a super ghostly sound out of an ordinary wooden ruler.

Take a flat ruler, or similar shaped piece of wood, and bore a hole at one end. Tie half a metre of string firmly to one end through the hole, and whirl the ruler around, slingwise, in a vertical circle. If you do it slowly you can make an eerie fluttering noise, which as you continue will die away and return. Increase the speed and the fluttering will become a low moaning.

Always play this game outside in a large open space so that you do not knock anything over, and never play it if other children are close to you.

What is the first thing ghosts do when they get in a car?

Fasten their sheet belts.

Game Number 60

ANKLE GUESSING

Get some of your friends to lie on the floor and cover them with a blanket so that only their feet and ankles stick out. The rest of your friends must then take a piece of paper and a pencil and write down whose ankles are sticking out and the order in which they appear.

Keep the guessers in a separate room whilst the people are getting under the blanket so that they cannot possibly see who is under there. To make it more difficult, get the players to remove their shoes and socks first so that just their bare feet stick out from the blanket.

Why are trousers always too short?

Two feet are always sticking out.

Game Number 61

CHECKSTONES

Checkstones was first played by the Ancient Greeks, since which time it has been known by various other names such as 'Chucks', 'Fivestones', 'Jackstones', 'Dulies' and 'Hucklebones'.

Whichever name you prefer, the game is still the same. You will need a small ball and five checks. There are all sorts of things that can be used as checkstones, such as pebbles, shells, cherry stones, even sugar lumps.

To play the game you take the checkstones in one hand and the ball in the other. Throw the five checkstones on the ground, then toss the ball in the air. Before you catch it, pick up a checkstone and put it down again.

Toss the ball into the air and this time pick up two checkstones and put them down again before you catch the ball. Continue this until you pick up all five checkstones. If you drop the ball at any time, or it falls before you have picked up and replaced the correct number of checkstones, you must start again from the beginning.

Game Number 62

DROP HANDKERCHIEF

Many of the games we play today originated from different parts of the world. This is a traditional Dutch game that children in Holland still play.

All but one of the players stand in a large circle holding hands. The remaining player walks around the outside of the circle and drops a handkerchief behind one member of the circle. That player must quickly turn around and catch it before it touches the ground. If he or she fails to catch it, the handkerchief must be picked up and the player must catch the one who dropped it. The player that dropped the handkerchief must run around the outside of the circle and if he or she gets a chance must dash into the other's place in the circle and hold hands with the others. He or she is then safe, and the player now with the handkerchief must drop it behind someone else and the game begins again.

What colours would you paint the sun and the wind?

The sun rose and the wind blue.

Game Number 63

TURNOVER TURTLE

The very simplest sounding games often turn out to be the hardest of all, just like this one!

Get your friend to lay flat on the ground. Face upwards or face downwards, whichever he or she prefers, with arms and legs stretched out like a turtle. Now you have to turn your friend over the other way, so that if the 'turtle' is lying on its front, you must turn it over on its back. That is really quite difficult. If you succeed, change over.

Who was the first to have a mobile home?

Yes, a turtle!

Game Number 64

SAUSAGES

For some unknown reason, the word SAUSAGES always makes people laugh. The object of this game is to try **not** to laugh. One person acts as questioner — he or she is allowed to laugh — and asks each of the other players in turn a question. Whatever the question is — *What do you hang on a Christmas tree?* — *What is your favourite pet? What do you wear in bed?* — *What twinkles in the sky at night?* — the person answering it must reply '**Sausages.**'

The first person to laugh becomes the questioner.

On the way to a water hole a zebra met 6 giraffes. Each giraffe had 2 apes hanging around its neck, and each ape had three birds sitting on its tail. How many animals were going to the water hole?

Only the zebra. All the rest were coming back from the water hole!

Game Number 65

HEADICKS AND PINTICKS

This game has such a marvellous name that it should be played throughout the year, although traditionally it is a Christmas game.

It is a kind of guessing game using matchsticks. Each player starts with ten matchsticks each and takes turns at playing. One player, without the opponent seeing, lays a matchstick on the forefinger with either the head pointing towards the fingernail (Headicks) or towards the palm (Pinticks). He or she then places the two hands together so that the matchstick is hidden between the two forefingers, and says 'Headicks or Pinticks?' If your opponent guesses correctly you give him or her the matchstick, if wrongly you take one of theirs. The winner is the person that ends up with all the matchsticks.

What should you do with old fingernails?

File them.

Game Number 66

SILLY SHOPPING

All the players sit in a circle. The first player begins the game by saying:

'On Saturday I went to the Supermarket and bought three baboons.'

The next player must then add on his or her purchase saying:

'On Saturday I went shopping and bought three baboons and a washing-up bowl.'

The next player adds on yet another purchase:

'On Saturday I went shopping and I bought three baboons, a washing-up bowl and half-a-dozen kippers.'

and so on:

'On Saturday I went shopping and I bought three baboons, a washing-up bowl, half-a-dozen kippers and a packet of soap flakes.'

So the game continues, building up the list of purchases until someone forgets one of them and is disqualified. The winner is the last one left.

What is an easy way to make your money bigger before you go shopping?

Put it under a magnifying glass.

Game Number 67

BLINDMAN'S BELL

To play this game you will need a large flat open space and a referee to keep an eye on everyone.

Collect everybody together and blindfold them all **except one**. The one remaining person is given a small handbell and becomes the bellringer. Who ever has the bell must run in and out of all the other players whilst they try to catch him or her by following the sound. Whoever catches the bellringer, changes places. If you do not have a bell, use a rattle or a tin can with a pebble inside.

Why are oranges like bells?

You can peel (peal) both of them.

Game Number 68

CIRCULAR SITTING

You need as many people as possible for this game. You might even be able to establish a new world record too!

Get everybody in a large circle. Everyone must place their hands on the hips of the person in front of them. On the command of 'SIT!' everyone must sit down on the knees of the person behind. If it is done properly each member of the sitting circle should be able to lift their arms into the air leaving no visible signs of support. Really advanced circles can try walking.

The world record for the most number of people in a sitting circle is 1,496, which was established in 1982. Can you beat that?

What is the difference between a banana and a bell?

You can only peel (peal) the banana once!

Game Number 69

LONG TERRACE

There's another good game to play with a large group of people.

You need a referee, and a player to be the 'Clapper'. Then everyone else needs to choose a partner, and stand in a long line immediately in front of each other, each pair about two metres apart. In the middle of the two rows is the 'Clapper', who has a soft sponge ball or bean bag.

On the word 'GO!' from the referee, the bottom pair have to run on the outside of the rows to the top end of the lines without being hit by the 'Clapper', who will try and throw the ball at them. If the 'Clapper' hits a runner, they change places. If you have a couple of extra people, put them outside the lines to catch the ball and return it to the 'Clapper' as quickly as possible.

Game Number 70

MUSICAL STICK

This game is always very popular with young children, so if you are organising a party for younger brothers or sisters then be sure to include this.

All the players must stand in a very large circle, and one person is given a walking stick. Music should be played and stopped at various intervals, as with musical chairs (if you can play the piano so much the better, but a tape-recorder, record player, or radio will do) as the stick is passed around the circle each person must tap it three times on the floor before passing it on to the person next to them. Whoever is holding the stick when the music stops leaves the circle. The one person left at the end is the winner. Remember that every person must tap the stick three times on the floor every time it reaches them, If you have a large number of players, have two sticks, one going clockwise and one going anti-clockwise. Two people will have to leave the circle each time the music stops, unless some unfortunate player ends up with both sticks at once!

Game Number 71

CROSSING OUT THE LETTERS

For this game you will need four pages from a newspaper, or one for each player if there are more than four. They can be any four pages that have a lot of writing on them, not a page full of photographs! To make the game really fair you should have identical newspapers for each player, but that is not important.

Each player takes their page and a pencil, and on the word 'GO!' from you they must cross out all the letter 'A's' on their page. The aim of the game is to have crossed out more of the letters than any other player within a set period of time.

You can work through the alphabet, and if they all have different pages the winner will be the lucky person who has crossed out every letter on his or her page. To make the game more complicated you can get the players not only to cross out one letter, but also to cross out certain words — like 'The', 'and', 'to' or 'of'.

Game Number 72

IT BEGINS WITH....

This is a quiet party game that adults enjoy playing as well as children. Listed below are a number of categories and the idea is to choose a letter of the alphabet, 'T' for instance, and for each category find an example beginning with hat particular letter. For example, a river beginning with 'T' could be the **River Thames**, a vegetable could be a '**Turnip**', a country '**Tunisia**', a flower '**Tulip**', and so on. At the end of the game each player reads out his or her list. If you have a word on your list that nobody else has then you score a point. If another player has the same word then he or she must shout out, and you both cross it off your list. You may find that three other players wrote down '**Thames**', but nobody else had '**Turnip**' as their vegetable — so you would not score a point for your river, but you would for the vegetable.

Name a **RIVER** beginning with 'T'...............

Name a **VEGETABLE** beginning with 'T'...........

Name a **COUNTRY** beginning with 'T'..............

Name a **FLOWER** beginning with 'T'..............

Name a **TOWN** beginning with 'T'................

Name a **TREE** beginning with 'T'................

Name a **PROFESSION** beginning with 'T'..........

Name an **ARTICLE OF CLOTHING** beginning with 'T'..........

Give a **BOY'S NAME** beginning with 'T'..........

Give a **GIRL's NAME** beginning with 'T'..........

Name an **ANIMAL** beginning with 'T'.............

Which newspapers do cows read?

The Daily Moos.

101

Game Number 73

ANIMAL NOISES

There is a very famous man called **Percy Edwards** who has made a career out of making animal noises. He can imitate any kind of animal or bird you care to mention. How clever are you at imitating animals? Do you, for example, know what sound a giraffe makes? Well, it would be easy to imitate because it cannot make any sound at all!

Here are some animal sounds that you can attempt to make. Write them down on pieces of card and drop them into a hat. Each player must then draw out a card in turn and make the noise that the card says. If the other players can identify the animal the imitator wins a point.

1. A puppy crying.
2. A pigeon cooing.
3. A cat miaowing.
4. A dog barking.
5. A lion roaring.
6. A crocodile snapping its jaws.

7. A snake hissing.
8. A mouse squeaking.
9. A rhinoceros bellowing.
10. A peacock screeching.
11. A sheep bleating.
12. A duck quacking.
13. A pig grunting.
14. A horse whinnying.
15. An elephant trumpeting.
16. A goose honking.
17. A chicken laying an egg.
18. A duck quacking.
19. A lion roaring.
20. A cat purring.

What do you get if you cross a chicken with a guitar?

A chicken that plays a tune when you pluck it.

Game Number 74

BALL AND HAT

Play this game outside, but with an old hat just in case it gets dirty! Place the hat upside down on the ground and stand about a metre away. The rest of the players must stand around you with one hand touching you.

Take a soft foam ball or bean bag and throw it into the hat. If you manage to get it in, all the other players must run off in different directions while you run to the cap and take the ball out. The moment you have picked up the ball, shout '**STOP!**' Everyone must stop immediately and stand still. You must then throw the ball or bean bag at someone — if you hit them it is their turn to throw the ball into the cap. If you miss, then you must start again.

If a player throws the ball at the hat and misses then someone else must have a go.

What did the scarf say to the hat?

'You go on ahead, I'll just hang around.'

Game Number 75

NINE MEN'S MORRIS

This development of Noughts and Crosses is another of those traditional English games which now have variations all over the world. For this game you will need to make yourself a board. Take a piece of cardboard about 20 cms square and copy this design on it. You can decorate and colour the board as you wish.

Each player has 9 buttons or tiddlywinks, a different colour for each player so that you can easily identify them. Take it in turns to lay a button down on the board on one of the 24 dots, the object of the game being to get three buttons in a straight line. The other player has to try and stop this and get three of his own in a line.

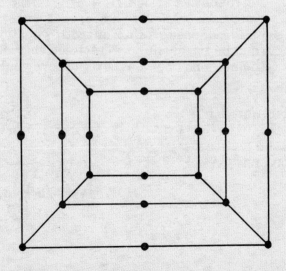

Game Number 76

CLOCK WHIRL

Just for fun, here is one of those daft games which is really not as easy as it sounds.

Place your right thumb on the ground and run round like a clock. How many times can you do this without falling over? Now try it in the opposite direction with your left thumb. Be careful not to tread on your thumb — no-one would ever believe you!

What time is it when a clock strikes thirteen?

Time to get the clock fixed.

When do clocks die?

When their time is up.

Game Number 77

ALPHAHOP

Find a large open space and hop, in very large letters, your name. Be grateful you were not christened **Wilberforce Montmorency Charlemagne Winklepicker the Third**!

Now gather your friends together and spell out any name or word that you like by hopping it out. As soon as they think they know what the word is they must shout it out. If the person is correct they take their turn at hopping out a word.

What belongs to you, but is used more by other people?

Your name.

LONG JUMPS

How far can you jump? To find out, lay a piece of string on the ground. Stand with your toes touching the string, bend your knees and jump. Place another length of string or a stick wherever you land, and measure the distance between the two points to see how far you have jumped.

Try jumping several more times to see if you can beat this distance. When you have jumped as far as you can, challenge a friend to jump and see which of you can jump the farthest.

Why did the baby ghost measure himself against a wall?

Because he wanted to know if he gruesome (grew some).

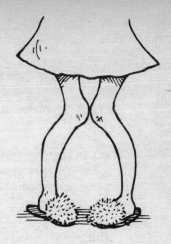

Game Number 79

KNOCK KNEES

Stand all the players in a circle and give the first player a balloon. The player must place the balloon between his or her knees and pass it on around the circle. The players can only use their knees and must not touch the balloon with their hands. If anyone drops the balloon they must leave the circle, and the winner is the person left with the balloon when everyone else is out.

There are many more fun games with balloons. One which always causes amusement at parties is really a naughty practical joke. You fill a plastic paddling pool with blown-up balloons. A player is then blindfolded and helped into the pool of balloons, having first had his shoes and socks removed. He is told that he has one minute to burst as many balloons as he can without using his hands. As he is blindfolded, what he will not see is that everyone in the room silently creeps up and removes all the balloons! The poor victim will stamp around in the empty space for a long time wondering why no balloons are bursting!

Game Number 80

BALL RACE

You will need one of those super bouncy balls for this game, the kind that are made of very hard rubber and will bounce to great heights.

Get your friend to hold the ball at shoulder height and drop the ball onto the ground. How many times can you run round your friend before the ball stops bouncing? Then it is your turn to drop it. If the ball is dropped from roughly the same height it should bounce the same number of times. Whoever clocks up the most number of runs is the winner. This is a good game to play in the playground because a nice hard surface is needed to drop the ball on.

What is the beginning of eternity,
The end of time and space,
The beginning of every end,
And the end of every race?

The letter E.

Game Number 81

DOG AND BONE

You will need a circle on the ground for this game. You could perhaps use a hoop, a circle of pebbles, or even chalk a circle on the ground.

One of the players takes the part of the 'dog' and places an object as his 'bone' in the centre of the circle. This can be a bar of chocolate, a handkerchief, or even a cardboard bone.

The two players stand on opposite sides of the circle and the dog challenges the other player to steal the bone. The player must try and make a grab at the bone and run off with it, whilst the dog attempts to catch him. If the dog catches the other player, then the two change over.

The game can be played another way. Have two circles on the ground and both players pretend to be dogs. The bone will be in the centre of one circle guarded by the dog, whilst the second player must attempt to grab the bone and get it into his or her own circle before getting caught. If the dog is successful in stealing the bone he must guard his own circle, whilst the other dog attempts to grab the bone back, and so the game continues.

Game Number 82

THE PICTURE FRAME GAME

This hilarious game is quite simple to set up. All you need is an old picture frame, or you can even make one by cutting one out of a large square of cardboard.

The players all sit facing the frame, as you hold it up to your face so that you are framed. Without laughing or smiling, you must try and look as serious as possible and keep perfectly still, just like a portrait in an art gallery. The more serious you look, the more your friends will laugh. They must try all they can to make you laugh too! They can pull funny faces, tell you jokes, make silly noises, or recite humorous poems, but whatever happens you must keep a straight face. If you laugh, one of the other players must take your place behind the frame.

What person tries to make you smile most of the time?

A photographer.

What did Cinderella say when her photographs didn't arrive?

'Some day my prints will come.'

Game Number 83

BLIND MAN'S GUESSING

When you are travelling along the same road every day, perhaps on the bus to school, the route becomes very familiar to you and can get very boring. If you find that you have to do a boring journey like that, then turn it into a game — it's much more interesting.

With your friend, take it in turns to close your eyes for two minutes at a time. The player with closed eyes must try and imagine the journey carefully, paying attention to when corners are turned, when you stop (perhaps at traffic lights and so on). After about two minutes the other player can ask a question such as *'What have we just passed?'* or *'What is ahead of us on the left?'* or *'Which road have we just turned into?'* and the player with closed eyes must answer the question before opening them. Score ten points if your guess is exactly right, 5 points if the landmark mentioned is within sight, and nothing if the guess is way out. Change places and let the other player guess.

An alternative version is to decide upon a particular landmark first, such as a church or a particular shop, and the player must close his or her eyes and when they think the landmark has been reached should shout 'NOW!' Points are scored as before.

Game Number 84

UMBRELLA TOSS

Here is an ideal game for a rainy day, if you can find an umbrella that isn't being used!

Open up the umbrella and stand it with the handle pointing upwards. The players stand about 5 metres away from the umbrella and take it in turns to bounce ping-pong balls into it. Every time a player throws a ping-pong ball and gets it to stay in the umbrella with it bouncing once and only once on its way there, he or she scores a point. After each player has had ten throws, the player with the highest score wins.

If you happen to be superstitious, you might believe that it is unlucky to open up an umbrella indoors. If so, place a dish or bowl on the floor instead.

Game Number 85

ROLLING ROUND THE WORLD

For this game you will need a marble for each team and two small bowls. An enamel bowl is best if you can get one, but any bowl or basin will do.

The players are divided into two teams of equal numbers. The teams are lined up into two rows, and the first player in each row is given a bowl and a marble. Each member of the team must stand in a line **behind** each other. On the shout of 'GO!' the player with the bowl must spin the marble round the inside of the basin and, keeping it spinning, turn round and pass it on to the player behind him. The basin continues to be passed like this down the row, to the end and back again to the leader. The marble must be kept spinning the whole time. If at any point the marble spins out of the bowl, it must be returned to the leader and spun again. The winning team is the first to finish, with the bowl returned to the leader and the marble still spinning.

If eight children and five dogs
stood under one umbrella,
why didn't any of them get wet?

Because it wasn't raining.

Game Number 86

LOGGATS

A loggat is a piece of wood which people in the country used to throw at fruit trees to knock off fruit that they could not reach. Children have played with loggats for centuries, although Henry VIII banned the game in the sixteenth century. It was revived again during the reign of Elizabeth I.

Nobody knows quite what shape loggats were, but you can use pieces of wood 15 cms by 5 cms, decorated with different colours for each player. To play the game, fix a stake in the ground and stand about three metres away. Take it in turns to throw loggats at the stake, the one that lands nearest wins a point. The first to score 20 points is the loggat champion.

Game Number 87

KNEESY

Choose a very small space in which to play this game, say a ten metre square or circle, and keep within that area. The object of the game is for your friend to chase you and try and touch you **behind the knee**. If you are touched, change over and try to touch him or her behind the knee. This game is always good fun, and not as easy as it sounds. Remember that the game is much more exciting if you play it in a small space, and even more fun if three or four of you play together, each of you trying to touch one person.

If a boy broke his knee, where could he get a new one?

At the butcher's shop where they sell kidneys.

Game Number 88

UNCLE JOSHUA

This old American game is perfect if you are camping and sitting around your campfire in the evening as it's beginning to get cold. The game is based around the verse of an old song:

'My Uncle Joshua died last night.'
'That's too bad; how did he die?'
'With one eye shut and his mouth awry,
One foot held high and waving goodbye.'

The players sit in a circle and the leader begins by saying to Player Number 2 *'My Uncle Joshua died last night.'* Player Number 2 replies, *'That's too bad; how did he die?'* *'With one eye shut,'* says the leader, closing one eye as he says it. The leader will now keep his eye shut until the end of the game.

It is now Player Number 2's turn and he turns to Player Number 3 and says, *'My Uncle Joshua died last night,'* gets the reply *'That's too bad; how did he die?'* and answers *'With one eye shut'* at which point he too closes his eye, whereupon it becomes player Number 3's turn. This goes on all around the circle until all the players are sitting with one eye shut. The leader then begins again, and says to Player Number 2, *'My Uncle Joshua died last night.'* Player Number 2 again replies, *'That's too bad, how did he die?'* but this time gets the answer, *'With one eye shut and his mouth awry.'* At this point the leader screws up his mouth, and keeps it screwed up for the rest of the game, while it now becomes Player Number 2's turn.

So this goes on around the group until everyone has one eye shut and their mouths screwed up. After four rounds all players will also have one foot held high and will be waving goodbye. Any player who gives the wrong answer or is caught opening an eye, or failing to wave goodbye, drops out of the circle. With a little luck, nobody will have to drop out and everybody will be a winner.

Game Number 89

SPILL THE BEANS

If you are having a party this is a good introducing game to get your guests talking to each other and relaxed. As each person arrives give them 5 dried beans or peas. They must then mingle with the others and ask them various questions and try and get them to say 'Yes' or 'No'. If they succeed, they must give the person one of their beans. The first person to successfully get rid of all his or her beans is the winner.

Remember that people will be asking you questions too, so be sure not to say 'Yes' or 'No', otherwise you could end up with a handful of beans.

What kind of beans won't grow in your garden?

Jelly beans.

How many beans can you put in an empty pocket?

One, after that it isn't empty.

Game Number 90

DOUBLE DUTCH

If you are good at skipping you will enjoy this tricky game.

Two skipping ropes are used with a person at each end holding the rope in either hand and turning the ropes alternately. The skipper must skip over each rope in turn. A more difficult version is to have one long rope which who people turn, while the skipper has a short rope which is turned inside the long one. This means the skipper has to keep turning his or her own rope and at the same time skip over the long rope. It's awkward, but it can be done!

Why do we sometimes call the Middle Ages the Dark Ages?

Because there were so many nights (knights).

PLAYING PAIRS

Take two packs of playing cards and spread them face down all over the floor. The players must sit around the edge of the cards in a large circle, and take it in turns to pick up two cards. If the cards they pick up are a matching pair, either two Kings, two Aces, two threes, two fours, or whatever (they don't have to be of the same suit) they keep the pair and have another go. If the two cards are different they must be laid face downwards again, and the next player takes a turn.

The object is to collect as many pairs as you can. If you have a good memory, you will remember where certain cards have been laid. For example, you may have picked up a seven and a nine on your last go, and now you have picked up another seven this time — if you can remember where you laid the seven before you will have a pair. This game is excellent for improving your memory!

Why are cards like wolves?

Because they belong to a pack.

Game Number 92

CHAIN TAG

This is like an ordinary game of tag in which one person is chosen as 'It' and has to catch all the others, but there is a slight variation.

One player is 'It', but when he or she catches another player they both hold hands and together try and catch someone else. The next person they catch joins hand with them, and so this carries on until there is a long chain trying to catch the few remaining people. On no account must anyone let go. Only the players at each end of the chain can tag.

To make **Chain Tag** even more difficult, play it in a space where there are lots of trees, pillars or other obstacles to get in the way.

> **What is nothing but holes tied to holes, yet is as strong as iron?**

A chain.

Game Number 93

FEELY-BAG

You can have some horrible fun with this game, which is not for the squeamish to play!

You will need a cloth bag with a drawstring around the top, the kind that people often keep plimsolls or sports shoes in. You can make one quite simply yourself if you do not have one. Get two pieces of cloth, both about 40 cms × 30 cms and sew three sides together to make a bag. The top of the bag should be turned over with a hem, and sewn all the way round, leaving a 2 cm gap that is not sewn up. Thread a string through the hem and you will have a drawstring bag. Get an adult to help you if you cannot sew.

To play the game you place a number of objects inside the bag, and challenge your friends to put their hands in the bag and guess what the objects are. When they have their hand in the bag, pull the draw-string so that it tightens the bag around their wrist, then they will not be able to look inside the bag.

There are a great number of objects that you can put in the bag which feel peculiar when they cannot be seen. A grape, a jelly baby, a piece of wool, a piece of cotton wool, a lump of cheese . . . and whoever can guess what all the objects are is the winner.

Which trees do fortune tellers look at?

Palms.

HOPSCOTCH

This is a game that your parents and grand-parents probably played when they were children. Mark out this figure on the ground, each of the ten squares is about 50 cms wide. You can chalk it out on the playground, but the best place to play is on the beach, particularly when the tide is low and the sand is wet and firm.

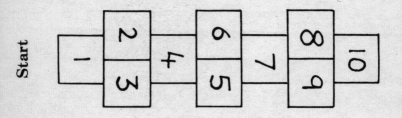

The players line up in turn at the starting line, and throw a pebble into one of the squares. If the pebble lands on one of the lines or falls outside the playing area the turn doesn't count and that player goes to the back of the queue. If the pebble lands in one of the squares, the player must go to that square, hopping on every single square and touching the sand with both feet on every double square, pick up the pebble and mark his or her initials in the corner of that square. If as the hopper touches any of the lines the turn doesn't count.

The winner is the player with his or her initial in every square. If you wish you can play the game with each player first having to get the pebble to land in square one, then square two, and so on, through to square ten.

Game Number 95

SQUIGGLES

To play a game of '**Squiggles**' with your friend, you do just that — squiggle!

Take a sheet of paper and draw a squiggle:

Give the page to your friend, who must turn your squiggle into a picture:

Now it is your friend's turn to do a squiggle!

Game Number 96

GUESSING GAME

This is a good game to play if you are giving a party and have time to prepare it. The idea of the game is that you fill different containers with various objects and the players have to guess how many objects are in each container. They keep a list of their guesses and the player with the most correct answers is the winner. The game takes time to set up because you will need to do the counting beforehand to be sure of the correct answers!

Here are some ideas for containers and things to put in them:

A jam jar full of dried peas — *how many peas?*
A bottle full of coins — *how many coins?*
A bottle full of rubber bands — *how many?*
A coil of string — *how long is the string?*
A teapot packed with teabags — *how many teabags?*
A plastic bag full of peanuts — *how many peanuts?*
A seaside bucket full of shells — *how many shells?*
A box full of crayons and pencils — *how many?*
A plastic bottle filled to a certain level with water — *how much does it contain?*
An exercise book of note pad of paper — *how many pages?*
A box of matches — *how many matches?*

Game Number 97

CRACKERS

If you are crackers you might attempt this game!

Give two players a plate with one cream cracker on it. Tell them that they must eat the cream cracker using only a knife and fork, and must not touch them with their fingers. The first person to eat his or her cream cracker in this way is the winner.

For the professional cream cracker eater there is an even tougher game. Challenge a friend to eat and swallow three cream crackers without having a drink while doing so. Both begin eating the cream crackers at the same time (you can use your fingers for this) and the one that finishes them first is the winner and can have a long drink of orange juice!

It has been said that this game is impossible and that **nobody** can eat three cream crackers without having a drink in between. Is this true?

If you crossed ducks and cows, what could you have?

Cream quackers.

Game Number 98

SHADOW CHARADES

This is a popular Victorian version of charades. Before the game can be played a large white sheet must be hung across the room. Get an adult to pin it to the ceiling for you. Weight the sheet at the bottom so that it keeps the screen you have now made perfectly tight. You will find that if you stand a lamp on one side of the sheet, from the other side it will appear like a big cinema screen!

Sit all your players on the outside of the screen, turn on the lamp with the rest of the room in darkness, and you are ready to begin. Divide the players into two teams. Each team must be given some pieces of paper on which you have written the title of a nursery rhyme, a book or television programme. Taking it in turns, two or three each team must go behind the screen and mime what is written on their paper. The other team must guess what is being mimed. Because they are performing their mime between the light and the sheet, the other team will be able to watch a shadow version of their charade.

Here are some nursery rhymes you could mime:

> *Mary had a little lamb.*
> *Humpty Dumpty.*
> *Polly Put the kettle on.*
> *Ding dong bell.*
> *Jack and Jill.*
> *Sing a song of sixpence.*

Game Number 99

DRAGON'S TAIL

You can have as many players as you wish for this game. As you play it you will discover how difficult it must have been for a dragon trying to catch its own tail!

Pretend that you are all part of a dragon's body by standing in a long line, each clasping your hands around the waist of the person in front of you. Tuck a handkerchief in the belt of the last person — the tail. The head of the line has to try and catch this handkerchief, while the tail of the line tries to keep out of the way. Everybody must hang on tightly and not let go.

If the person at the head successfully catches the handkerchief, he or she then becomes the tail and the next player in the line becomes the head. This way everybody gets a turn.

How can you calm down an angry dragon breathing fire?

Throw water at him and he will let off steam.

Why do dragons sleep during the day?

So that they can fight knights.

CLOCKING CARS

The next time you are on a car journey, play a game of clocking cars. You can play this game on your own, but it is more fun with a friend.

Take it in turns at looking at car numbers on the road, the first player looks at the first car that passes, the second player the second, and so on. The idea is to collect numbers from one to twelve. If the first car that passes has the number 418 the first player counts one, because the number had a one in it. If the number had been, for example, 537 the player would have to wait until his next turn.

The second player then has to look for a car with a one in the number. When looking for 10, 11, 12 the number must be together on the number plate — 192 would not count as 12, but 129 would.

The first player to get around the clock from one to twelve is the winner.

What kind of car can drive over water?

Any kind if there is a bridge.

Game Number 101

YOUR FAVOURITE GAME

Write your favourite game on this page and then send it to the National Playing Fields Association as Prince Philip suggests at the beginning of the book.

AFTERWORD

Prince Philip is the President of the National Playing Fields Association. What does NPFA do? And why is it important?

We live in a world designed and built for adults by adults.

Children must live in this world too.

It is the world in which they have to grow.

A vital part of that growing up process is play. For children play is not trivial or unimportant. It is an integral part of their healthy development.

It is in their play that children learn about life and about living — their preparation for their future. Without it the deprived child develops into the deprived adult.

Children *need* to play and have the *right* to grow and develop in freedom and in safety.

We call our world 'the developed world.'

HOW DO CHILDREN SEE IT?

They see:
- high rise flats
- estates with postage-stamp gardens
- signs 'Keep off the Grass' — 'No Ball Games Here'
- more space for cars than for children.

It is not just the environment which has become alien, almost hostile, to children but people as well. We have separated children from adults in their work, their education and their leisure.

We are destroying their play world. We are placing our children at risk.

In doing so we place our future at risk.

The simple needs are often forgotten.

THE NATIONAL PLAYING FIELDS ASSOCIATION.

Fifty years ago **NPFA** was established with a simple mandate: every child has a right to play.

Nothing could be simpler.

Yet, our society is losing sight of this simple idea.

NPFA has not, and is now one of the most effective voices for better play provision.

It is not a fashionable cause. It is not an emotional cause.

It is a cause concerned with the bed-rock on which our society is founded.

A concern for how children grow and develop is a concern for the future and the shape our society will take.

NPFA believes that we are failing our children, ourselves and our future in this key area.

It is still not too late though the call for action grows more urgent.

THE REAL NEEDS.

In providing real play opportunities we can no longer salve our consciences by giving expensive toys and play equipment.

Just to provide swings and roundabouts is only scratching at the surface of children's real needs.

It is not just a question of space and equipment.

Children also need:
- to be creative
- to be stimulated and challenged
- to be involved in all aspects of life.

Otherwise they will seek their excitement in other ways.

Most of all **NPFA** believes children need people.

Children need the care and involvement of adults in their play.

This means nothing less than a total change of attitudes. Bringing children — and their play — into the centre of our lives and thinking.

When we plan for children we plan for our future.

NPFA believes this means fighting for children.
- fighting to give them space
- fighting to give them time to play
- fighting to give them opportunities for play
- fighting to involve people in their play.

Above all else:

NPFA is fighting for the child's right to play.

It means making the right choices in allocating our national resources.

Play is cost effective:
- it saves — repairing children's bodies and minds
- it saves — by lessening delinquency, violence and vandalism
- it saves — by preventing stress in families.

That is what **NPFA's** appeal for children's play is about.

It is the only organisation with the potential to fight effectively for children's play.

That is why we urgently need your help and support.

- to create a greater understanding of the value of play to children
- to persuade both public and private sectors of their responsibilities to children
- to improve the quantity and quality of play opportunites for children
- to support means of involving adults in the play — and therefore — the lives of children
- to search for new initiatives for children's play provision.

In fact:

<u>TO FIGHT FOR THE CHILD'S RIGHT TO PLAY.</u>

National Playing Fields Association,
25 Ovington Square, London, SW3 1LQ.
Telephone: 01-584-6445.

If you would like to receive a newsletter telling you about our new children's books, fill in the coupon with your name and address and send it to:

Gillian Osband,

Transworld Publishers Ltd,

Century House,

61–63 Uxbridge Road, Ealing,

London, W5 5SA

Name ....

Address ....

....

CHILDREN'S NEWSLETTER

All the books on the previous pages are available at your bookshop or can be ordered direct from Transworld Publishers Ltd., Cash Sales Dept. P.O. Box 11, Falmouth, Cornwall.

Please send full name and address together with cheque or postal order—no currency, and allow 45p per book to cover postage and packing (plus 20p each for additional copies).